# MANUEL DE FALLA
# TWO DANCES

*from 'The Three-Cornered Hat'*

*arranged for Guitar by*
Siegfried Behrend

1. Dance of the Miller
2. Dance of the Corregidor

# Chester Music

# DANCE OF THE MILLER

## From "The Three Cornered Hat"

Arranged for Guitar by
**SIEGFRIED BEHREND**

MANUEL DE FALLA

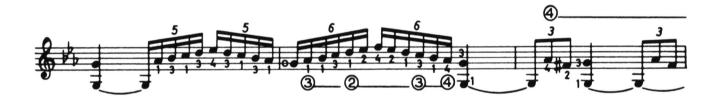

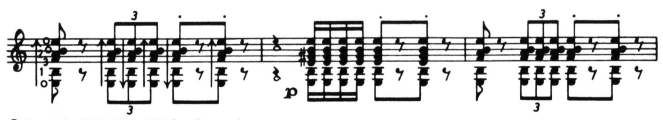

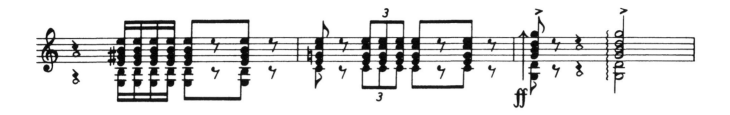

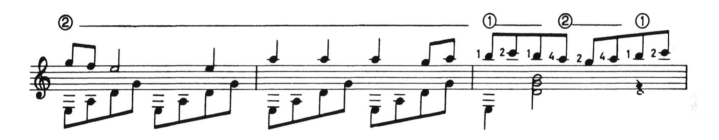

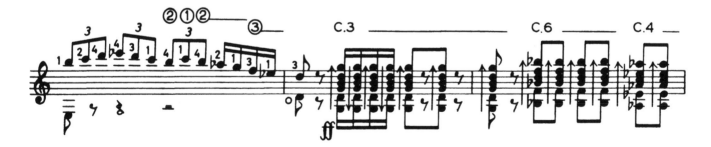

3

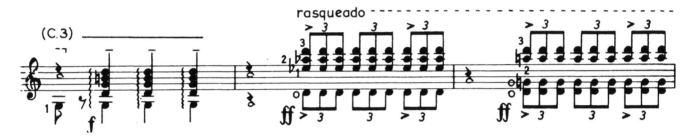

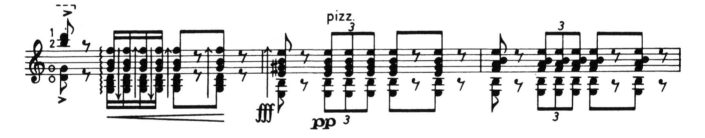

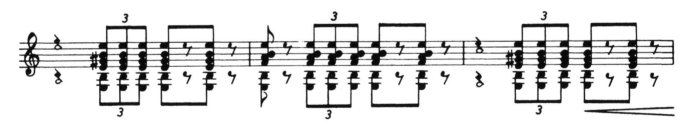

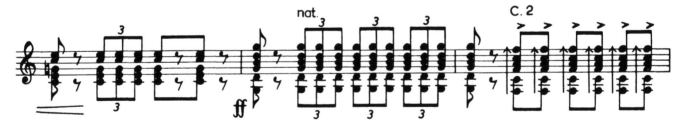

Lento
C.3

vivo

vivissimo

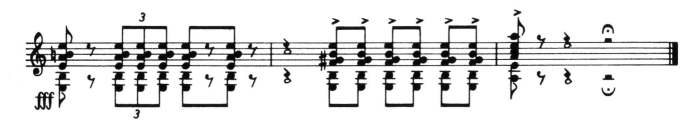

# DANCE OF THE CORREGIDOR

From "The Three Cornered Hat"

Arranged for Guitar by
SIEGFRIED BEHREND

MANUEL DE FALLA

Allegretto (♩ = 100)

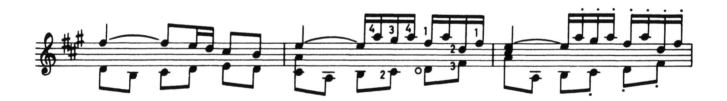

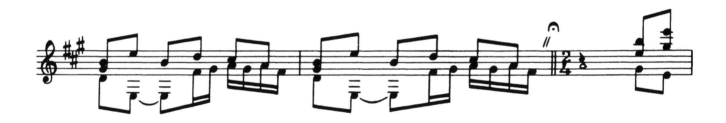